DO NOT
CALL
THE
TORTOISE

Gareth Howell-Jones

CONTENTS

PREFACE

And do not call the tortoise unworthy because she is not something else
(Walt Whitman)

A little while ago I came by chance upon a slightly different way of looking at the world which I called 'STA'. I had to call it something. The essays collected here were written from that perspective, and so I hope they may serve as a casual introduction. (It can be explored more fully at *www.sta-website.com* and in the book predictably entitled STA serialised at *www.sta-serial.com*)

STA could be described as a thought-experiment: how would the world appear to us if we looked at it squarely, without our social and cultural preconceptions? From this everyday experience which each of us can share, it builds a rational world-view that is surprising, heartening and quietly radical. But you mustn't take my word for it. The best advice is to try it yourself:

Sta et considera miracula; stand still and consider the wondrous things.

Whitman's tortoise has become STA's mascot. The worth of any creature or person must surely lie in its own being, and not in our expectations of it. The chasm between this idea and modern society's behaviour is so mesmerizingly deep and wide I've been drawn back to stare at it constantly. I hope that hasn't made me repetitive.

    This little book was published on Coleridge's 250th birthday – a small, ludicrously inadequate salute to Eng. Lit's most exhilarating, humane and multifarious contributor. His *The Eolian Harp* is a fitting accompaniment to Whitman:

> *O the one life within us and abroad,*
> *Which meets all motion and becomes its soul,*
> *A light in sound, a sound-like power in light,*
> *Rhythm in all thought, and joyance every where –*
> *Methinks it should have been impossible*
> *Not to love all things in a world so filled;*

STA – an Extract

'STA'

I was just walking dully along when, as usual, I turned and looked, and this time, to my surprise, said,
  'STA'

Everyone knows it's a good view – from Oxford Road below the castle wall, across the main car-park falling away to the twin hawthorns in flat Cae Mawr, Nine Acres, Ox Meadow, up to the farms and ancient woods that decorate the skirts of the Black Mountains. Not a grand panorama but an involving and companionable view – a sudden openness in contrast to the narrow streets of the town and the hedged lanes that surround it. Tourists stop to take pictures, hopelessly failing to capture what they see. It is probably unphotographable. But on this January morning, though the view was so familiar, I stopped too and took a picture.

It's a rotten photograph, much worse than the usual tourist pics. The sun flared suddenly while I was fumbling for my phone. But I took the photo anyway to remind me of the moment. Of course, the 'moment' was the moment before the moment in the picture but that doesn't really matter because even if I had pressed the button at exactly the right moment the resulting photo would have been only a photo – perhaps a lovely thing, but different from the thing I experienced. The camera never lies, but it doesn't tell much of the truth either. The liars are the people who tell you this is how it was, mistaking the shadow for the substance and trying to flog you a phantom of an experience rather than a real, genuine, lovely photograph. And this account which I'm trying to relate as honestly as I can is of course not the real experience, but that doesn't matter because that's not the point either – the story is not the point of the story. When (perhaps I should say 'if') I get to the point what you will have is the universe (or a portion of it) processed by me not the thing itself. Reading any book is a first-hand experience of a second-hand experience, but if it inspires or reminds you to explore the author's first-hand experience first-hand, it needn't be 'a load of crap'. I won't be an artfully unreliable narrator – that's a tiresome trick – just an inevitably, regretfully unreliable one.

I haven't looked at the picture again till now. Here it is.

Told you.

But I hadn't looked because I haven't needed reminding. I'm not likely to forget what I saw even if I've forgotten what it looked like.

It was a low-lying-skeins-of-mist-with-a-low-morning-sun-firing-through-them sort of thing. It was, anyway, breathtakingly beautiful and its evident ephemerality – the mist drifting, the clouds about the sun – doubtless heightened the beauty. The beauty itself wasn't the point (aesthetics never is) but it drew me in. In fact, the look of it wasn't the point either. The point was the thing itself – the thing behind the look. Just as a painting is a window to the thing behind, which the painter mustn't paint over.

Admittedly, the beauty of the view that startled me was having little effect on anyone else. One woman went past looking at a shopping-list, another her phone. A few cars busily drove by. Back in town some time later, people were gossiping in the café (as I might have been on another morning) or buying their papers and moaning at the news, warming themselves on a wintry day with the certainty of their opinions.

But I just said, 'STA'.

STA

ET CONSIDERA

MIRACULA DEI

I don't insist on the 'Dei'. How on Earth should I know? '*Sta et considera miracula naturae*' might have done just as well but that wasn't the quote. Stand still, and consider the wondrous works of God. [Footnote: I should explain that I do not habitually walk around speaking Latin. I had been struck by the verse (Job 37:14) when I read it and turned to see what the Latin Vulgate version was. I occasionally carve stone inscriptions which work better in Latin than in English. In a foreign language, they can aspire to an iconic, meditative quality which creates its own context – 'STA', while in English they just read like any other sign and, in this case – 'STAND STILL' – rather a silly one.] That's the job. So I did for a bit. And the wondrous works changed as the mist moved and the clouds moved and the sun came and went and all the works shuffled around a bit and became less aesthetically beautiful but suddenly no less wondrous.

And that was it, the epiphany, if that's not too high a word. That, I think, is how they generally work, these days at least. No angels, no charred shrubbery, no extra lighting – the sun is always light enough. Just the world sitting there as normal and me finally seeing it. No disembodied hand materialized to write the meaning of it all on the castle walls or in the little notebook I carry round in case of such eventualities. So I made a few notes myself.

It was not a revelation so much as a prompt, alerting me to some things, bringing together thoughts and realisations scrawled in notebooks or stored in my memory, telling me nothing I hadn't already heard, but telling me so I listened.

Because the world is unimaginably complex, much of our thought that attempts to understand it has to be bureaucratic – allocating names to nameless things, understating reality in the hope of making it comprehensible, reducing the image so that it's not too big to send, organizing data into manageable files. Most of the taxonomies, the divisions we invent are not real, but it needn't be a dishonest process unless we tell ourselves it's true.

So, arranged for administrative convenience, this is what occurred to me that day after seeing the sun-through-skeins-of-mist thing:-

ORGANISED UNDER NINE HEADINGS,
A BRIEF SYNOPSIS OF THINGS SUDDENLY REALISED
ONE JANUARY 5TH,
IT BEING A SUNNY, MISTY MORNING

1. That this is it. This is what is. That this business of sun and mist and earth, the physicality of things, ephemeral as this manifestation may have been, is real and universal. That it is not contingent on anything else on earth. It just is. And, that being so – being certain, a sure foundation and the basis of everything we think and perceive – that it is what matters most. Nature is not a consolation for all the hardships of life; the world is not a stage built for humans to perform on. 'The morning shines, Nor heedeth Man's perverseness.'
This does not preclude the possibility of a further (deeper? higher? Select your most emotionally satisfying dimension) level of reality, nor does it confirm it. Nature stays mum. It just is.

2. That nature makes and makes unceasingly. Inanimate objects arranged into endless new patterns, and new life created – zillions of new forms every second for billions of years, and every one of them unique.

3. That we live mostly oblivious to all this. That, while every other creature lives exclusively attuned to this reality, we prefer to concentrate on the things we've made ourselves – shopping,

football, radio shows, nights out, political debates – which are seldom rooted in or even aware of the overarching and underlying reality. That the disconnection between our pre-occupations and those of the rest of the planet's inhabitants may suggest difficulties ahead.

4. That God is bewildered that we can't see all this. That God has put on the most incredible show, which we ignore so we can listen to *The Archers*. I do not at all insist on this – I have no idea whether there is a God of some sort or not – but that was the feel of the thing that day. 'And he marvelled because of their unbelief.'

5. That we are part of this reality and not separate in any way. 'The force that through the green fuse drives the flower Drives my green age.' That all that is happening around us is happening in us too because we're all the same stuff. That there is a potential sense of belonging latent in this, a sense of reassurance and homecoming, a sense of excitement at being involved, at joining the dance rather than standing by the wall making sly observations behind gloved hands.

6. That, this being what matters most, and our being unavoidably involved in it, all we have to do to possess and enjoy these feelings of belonging is to show willing. To say '*Fiat mihi*' and accept reality.

7. That nature is perfect. That it is so by definition, because any perspective other than universal nature's own must be personal, partial and frankly impertinent. That we may need to modify our personal notions of perfection accordingly.

8. That the uniqueness of each created thing makes everything fundamentally equal, and that the universe is based on egalitarianism rather than hierarchy, and individuality-with-interdependence rather than common identity or atomization.

9. That this being what is and universal, our acceptance of it, our assenting to it is the same thing as the capacity for seeing connections and making whole – in other words, our imagination.

Ouf!

At some point, I'll need to examine all these claims, and see which of them make sense, and what, if anything, they mean. Will they give any clue to that perennial question: 'what shall we do with our time?' But for now I need a break. I imagine you may do too.

So I took a day off, and walked the hills above Rhulen to the Mawn Pool, and picked whinberries and made delicious pies of them.

(This is the opening chapter of the book STA, which is being published online in instalments at www.sta-serial.com. The claims above are indeed examined — with surprising consequences. There are poems, pictures and speculations, with contributions from Tolstoy, Siouxsie Sioux, Rembrandt, Jesus, Virginia Woolf among others. Paddington Bear gets to meet Cezanne. Why make art? What is my identity? What inspires a woodlouse? STA's intentions are serious but its method playful. Its core is the recognition that the 'simple' things of nature — hills, people, warthogs, whinberries — have a much deeper reality than the social conventions and technology that obsess us. Knowing this gives us agency and hope. 'The world is a mirror of infinite beauty,' sings Traherne. He may well be right but we mustn't take his, or anyone else's, word for it — we each need to stand still and consider for ourselves.)

BURNING BUSHES

One afternoon, many years ago, a man was minding some sheep on a hill when a nearby bush burst into flame. Then it started talking to him. This, it transpired, was the work of God (who else?) who chose this unusual floral disguise to protect the shepherd (Moses) from the full force of His Divine Reality. "Thou canst not see my face: for there shalt no man see me, and live."

None of us can see the universal. But we can look at the particular – the living details of the universe like the burning bush – and find the universal there, because every particular contains the universal. Every bush is a burning bush, aflame with the motive and creative power of the world. And as I stare at this rose in my garden I see both the rose and the universe-in-the-rose, because a rose cannot exist in isolation: all life is interconnected, sprung from the same source, that single cell in which all life on earth began. Religions can miss this, overleaping the particular in their eager search for some Ultimate State or Being; science too can miss it, littling down to the mechanisms in the persistent belief that a living thing can be dissected and understood as though the whole were no more than the sum of its own parts.

Every bush is a burning bush. That is to say that every creature, every person we meet has the spark that is elsewhere the swift's acrobatics, the peacock's display, the ant's resilience, the yew's endurance, the chickweed's fecundity, Shakespeare's verse. Every one is a specific part of the whole. For all our glittering variety, each deep down is the other.

Blake cries, 'Everything that lives is holy,' and, as the etymology shows, 'holy' incorporates a sense both of health and of wholeness. Everything is made perfect and is part of an entirely interdependent system, which is not merely a collection of those parts but a single unity revealing itself in more and more ways as it splits into infinite new forms. It is not a hierarchy, not a drama with protagonist and chorus; *everything* that lives is holy.

So here I am in the middle of this fire-field, life incandescent but unconsumed, crackling all around me. Visions don't occur *beyond* the lived world, but through it: reality itself is miraculous.

If all this sounds a bit mystical, it is a down-to-earth, bread-and-butter mysticism, found not in vagueness and obfuscation, but in a blackbird's egg, a blade of grass, a person, mysteries so commonplace we take them for entitlements, miracles we have analysed so deeply we think we have explained when we have only described them.

These living creatures all around me, new manifestations of the single life, new torches kindled from the same fire, unique, inexplicable, nameless miracles are real and replete, and, because I am one of them, as they flood my perceptions and spur my mind to recreate them in thoughts, sensations and feelings, so am I.

No explanations or assessments are needed in any case. Although we cannot hold such cogent conversations with the universal as Moses talking to that flaming bramble-patch, we can acknowledge its presence and the influence of this necessary reality in our lives. We are part of the same unity and share an affinity with every other part. It is the very basis of our existence, and all that we need to know.

P.S. Moses, along the way, asks God who he is and receives for an answer the wisest thing God or anyone else ever said: 'I am that I am'. If we were all content with that true description of ourselves and not tempted to fabricate an identity, how much quieter and more tolerant, how much more deeply engaged with realities than with names the world would be!

NULL
IUS *
IN * V
ERBA

SEEINGS – 1

I am gazing out of my bedroom at the trees. One branch is broken and the dying leaves shine out. My brain logs the data: 'yellow against the green'.

But as I look at that yellow, think how to describe it (custard mustard gold bananas) it deepens, orange flares from below as tea suffuses richer depths in brewing. The light hasn't warmed to intensify the colour; the change is in my brain, which has gone beyond its instinctual habit of comparison, the hasty assessment which will usually do, to acknowledge this specific experience, the uniqueness of these leaves right now.

We have evolved to see what we expect – in that sense, prejudice is our inheritance – but if we look just a little longer, take a moment more . . . we can override our default simplicity, and pay due respect to the world outside our heads.

SEEING THE WOOD

In the spring of 1798, Wordsworth breezed through the Quantock woods moralising merrily:

> Come forth into the light of things,
> Let Nature be your Teacher.
>
> She has a world of ready wealth,
> Our minds and hearts to bless –
> Spontaneous wisdom breathed by health,
> Truth breathed by cheerfulness.

The Romantic poets were re-discovering our affinity with all living creatures. They looked upon the earth and saw that it was good. 'Sweet is the lore which Nature brings,' he beamed.

Exactly a hundred years later another poet, seeking in 'Nature a soft release/From men's unrest' also went for a sylvan stroll, but something had gone wrong. Wisdom, health and cheerfulness were nowhere to be found as

> Sycamore shoulders oak,
> Bines the slim sapling yoke,
> Ivy-spun halters choke
> Elms stout and tall.

The wood has become a vision of Hell where trees whip, throttle and poison one another. Has some dread catastrophe befallen sweet nature? No, it is just the same as before, but the poet, Thomas Hardy, has read Darwin and learnt about 'the struggle for existence' and 'survival of the fittest'.

These two phrases (the first Darwin's own, the second coined by Herbert Spencer but adopted by Darwin as a synonym for Natural Selection) have come to summarise the popular understanding of evolution and, more widely, the mood in which nature operates. They are believed to be 'scientific' and therefore 'true'. I do not for a moment question the theory of evolution which is accepted by all but the most pig-headed creationists, but these phrases are not science, they are metaphors.

Once scientists leave their labs and try to explain their findings to the public they are forced, like the rest of us, to use analogies and images, which are not strictly science itself but a form of story-telling and must be understood as such. When they speak of an electron's 'spin', they do not mean that the electron actually spins; when they use the jokey phrase 'junk DNA' to describe 90% of our make-up they tell us less about the molecule than their own preconceptions. Darwin is quite candid about this: 'I use the term Struggle for Existence in a large and metaphorical sense', but his audience and perhaps he himself began to be seduced by the imagery as much as by the technical data.

'The survival of the fittest' is a misleading phrase (and modern biologists avoid it). Survival isn't on offer – we all die. What is said to survive is the 'species' but species do not have a real existence –

they are, in Darwin's own words, 'artificial combinations made for convenience'. Only individuals are real, and none of them survives. Similarly, no creature evolves. Evolution by Natural Selection – the gradual privileging of advantageous over disadvantageous traits – can only be discerned in retrospect as a generalisation over many years. A creature with a seemingly 'favourable variation' may yet die long before it can breed; one with a variation that, after several generations, will prove 'injurious', may live its life and breed successfully. So, although Natural Selection brilliantly explains how we have come to be the creatures we are, proving all that Darwin hoped it would prove, it does not reflect the life lived by any individual. 'The survival of the fittest', is not a 'law' which acts inevitably like the Laws of Thermodynamics; it is best understood as historiography – a rule of thumb like 'Power tends to corrupt' or 'All empires fall' – true enough seen from a hazy Olympian perspective but irrelevant to the lives lived down on the ground, which are shaped by an unpredictable mix of genes, environment, will and chance.

'The struggle for existence', meanwhile, implies inevitable conflict. This again is misleading. I stopped in a lay-by just south of Llanbister last week. On the broad verge there I found forty different 'species' of wild flowers, and doubtless there were many more I'm too ignorant to distinguish. Are these beauties really engaged in a grim 'struggle for existence' that only the most sharp-elbowed will win, as Hardy glumly let himself believe? Surely if that were the case one would have emerged as victor after so many generations, but instead of a monoculture we have this wonderfully rich diversity. We do not evoke the 'struggle for existence' when we see a pregnant woman at a café table eating a toasted teacake, and yet these roadside flowers are doing much the same, absorbing nutrients and setting seed.

Darwin's vision of 'the great battle of life' was not constructed solely out of biological evidence. The story was already in the air. The previous century's drive to classify nature corralled unique creatures into 'species' and 'phyla' so that broad patterns could be traced until, at last, a narrative emerged from the mess of data. This story, repeated in various forms by philosophers, historians and politicians, told of conflict resolved into inevitable 'Progress', a tale supported by advances in science, and the triumph of the British Empire. All of this was exemplified by the Great Exhibition just a few years before *Origin of Species* appeared.

With human knowledge, politics and society chuffing along on the railroad to paradise, Darwin hopped aboard to tell us that all of creation was heading the same way: 'thus, from the war of nature, from famine and death, the most exalted object which we are capable of conceiving, namely, the production of the higher animals, distinctly follows. There is grandeur in this view of life … As Natural Selection works solely by and for the good of each being, all corporeal and mental endowments will tend to progress towards perfection.' He gives a quasi-scientific authority to what is little more than a popular mood. In fact, nature is only bumblingly Darwinian – there are plenty of diversions, distractions and dead-ends along the way. Natural Selection is not how things live; it is how abstractions and generalisations can be explained. As A.N.

Wilson writes, 'It is only by telling the tale that we create the illusion that there is a tale to tell'.

However, our popular understanding of evolution has grown out of the metaphors not the science itself. It has taken Natural Selection out of context as though it were specific and deterministic, and then applied this 'turbo-Darwinism' more broadly to society in capitalism and technology, both of which are predicated on struggle and victory. As this agonistic melodrama, broadcast 24/7 by a compliant media, dominates public life, so we justify it as somehow 'natural' behaviour with this threadbare Victorian imagery. (Darwin, of course, is not to blame for all of this, and certainly not to blame for the death camps and the forced sterilisations that resulted from his theory's extrapolation into human eugenics, but his slapdash metaphors encouraged the mad and unscrupulous in their perversions. As soon as we believe in the chimerical 'species', or equally illusory tropes like race and nationality, the precious life of each individual is in jeopardy.)

The truth is that we are all exceptional individuals, and have a random independence free of any 'laws' of evolution and the metaphors wrung from them. We do not 'struggle for existence', nor, sadly, do we 'progress towards perfection' – we just do the things we do because we're who we are.

And here, all around me on this summer evening are creatures doing exactly that. At my ear a wasp rasps insistently, gnawing at the deckchair for nest-paper; there are tiny, mazy flies who find some kind of food in the tall grass-flowers, and one floundering in my glass who, rescued on a fingertip and raised aloft to dry, cleans itself of sticky wine with the care of a groom for a thoroughbred. The grasses themselves still this calm evening are no less busy ripening their seeds. Ringlet butterflies oscillate wildly, a solitary bee darts around the roses, which are pumping out prodigious quantities of scent. Swifts silently gather their food, midges silently die in their craws. The cat sleeps on the man's lap, the man sits and looks at it all. Gut flora hectically process pasta.

If the Victorian metaphors are so misleading, how can we characterise this plenitude of life without merely substituting our zeitgeist for theirs? There *is* some struggle and competition certainly (the swifts and midges, for example; the rough grass that has smothered the strawberries), there is some mutual assistance (the rose and the bee, and who knows what intimate collaboration between the plants and mycorrhizal fungi), most of all there is peaceful co-existence without paying much practical attention to one another (the swifts and grass and rose and cat and wasp).

Each of us is doing our stuff, and most of it is the same – finding a place to be, keeping ourselves alive, eating, shitting, breeding, dying. We are all on the same trip engaged on similar business, out on our adventures, exploring the world around us, each unique but none of us isolated, all dependent in some way on the others. We are a motley crowd but banded together on the road like the Canterbury Pilgrims. And what astonishing stories each of us could tell – The Swift's Tale, The Rose's Tale, The First Bacterium's Tale, The Cat's Flea's Tale.

This pilgrimage of all living things may seem like tiresome whimsy, the most pathetic of fallacies, but it is no more anthropomorphic than Darwin's grim war-song. Indeed, representing real creatures rather than the abstractions of species and genus, this image of all creation roading together, beating the path between birth and death, is the most lifelike depiction of what is actually going on that I know, because the most important of Darwin's great discoveries was, after all, not Natural Selection, but Common Ancestry: 'probably all the organic beings which have ever lived on this earth have descended from some one primordial form, into which life was first breathed' – the astonishing realisation that inanimate matter burst into life just once in all the billions of years that anything has existed and that we are all equally the progeny of that moment. Although most philosophers and all politicians have ignored it, Common Ancestry – a scientific fact evident quite literally in our DNA – is a surer basis for our thinking, our culture and society than the video-game fantasy of battling towards some promised perfection. It tells instead a living lesson of kinship here and now, the unity of all creation.

Seventy years after Hardy's horror, Wendell Berry ventured back into the woods: 'As I go in under the trees, dependably, almost at once, and by nothing I do, things fall into place. ... I feel my life take its place among the lives – the trees, the annual plants, the animals and birds, the living of all these and the dead – that go and have gone to make the life of the earth.' We are, I suspect, most fulfilled, most ourselves, not by an inward exploration of our psyches, nor by a quest for knowledge and power, but by this simple acknowledgement of our place in this interdependent, interpenetrative world.

GWNEW
CH * Y *
PETHA
U * BYC
HAIN *

SEEINGS – 2

In July 1797, Coleridge was living with his wife and baby son in Somerset. Friends were down – the Wordsworths from Dorset, Charles Lamb from London – promising a week of walking, talking, poetry, politics and fellowship. But that morning, Sara spilt a pan of hot milk down his leg; so, as the others tramped away up and over the Quantocks, the invalid sat 'imprisoned' in the garden, envying them the hills and combes and water-falls.

Then he stopped and considered his surroundings:

> 'Nor in this bower,
> This little lime-tree bower, have I not mark'd
> Much that has sooth'd me. Pale beneath the blaze
> Hung the transparent foliage; and I watch'd
> Some broad and sunny leaf, and lov'd to see
> The shadow of the leaf and stem above
> Dappling its sunshine!'

A nothing – a leaf with a shadow on it, just the leaf that happens to be before his eyes and for that sole reason worth his acknowledgement. This is a rare quality of witness; not the Enlightenment botanist's careful research, nor the glance of earlier poets looking for material to reflect their mood. His floating mind is alert but not focussed, all its doors and windows open. He pays the leaf its due respect, the nod from one chance creature to another – it exists and that's enough.

Dore Abbey has the most beautiful lime I know, its leaves pale beneath the blaze and dappled just like Coleridge's. You can disappear inside it. The thick, sweet scent is heavy and heady there, the thrum of the bees an incantation.

But words, like the films and pictures I took, are shadows of experience. Go there yourself in July!

AN IGNORANT MAN WRITES AN UNINFORMATIVE ESSAY

My laptop is bursting with information it longs for me to know. I am amazed it keeps so slender when it is pregnant with omniscience. I should probably ask it something but I'm getting rather tired of knowledge.

Here is a random, by no means comprehensive, selection of things I know: that the earth orbits the sun, the location of Tierra del Fuego, Boyle's Law of Gases, the causes of the Franco-Prussian War, the winner of the F.A. Cup in 1927 etc etc etc etc. The Royal Society mightn't think much of this list. 'Nullius in verba' is their motto – 'Take nobody's word for it' – and I see their point. This is just stuff someone or other has told me, which I then repeat. It's high-toned gossip really. There's not much on the list I could confirm without relying on someone else's data – I suppose I could go to Tierra del Fuego but ....

And suppose it were all untrue; suppose, for example, Copernicus was wrong and all his predecessors right: the rain would still fall, the crops grow, people love or murder one another. If it's all an astonishingly elaborate hoax, well, it wouldn't make much difference. I can't imagine any other creature stocking up with this kind of stuff, because none of it has much to do with life. Information and interpretations only distance us from being. They slip a sheath of explanation over our lives as though to protect us from infection by immediacy. It is prophylactic learning.

But we're convinced that knowledge of this sort is important and so give in to our laptops' importunities, drenching ourselves in a flood of information, much of it thrilling or thought-provoking, much of it opinion in fancy-dress, much of it untrue. Numbers always lend a bit of heft, so we swallow statistics and the results of surveys that sound 'scientific'. We think the precision of these numbers gives authority, and so we trust whatever-it-is on the other side of our screen and, in doing so, surrender a little of our precious independence.

Yesterday, a page on the BBC website told me to 'Find out what the weather is doing where you are.' Luckily my house has doors and windows.

In defiance of the deluge, I should like to make the case for the richness, necessity and inescapability of ignorance. Here, to provide some context is

An Incomplete Checklist of Things I Know I Don't Know About

1. The Future (pay no heed to the cocky predictions of economists, politicians, generals &c – they've been wrong many times before, and do not know. They're only on your screens to fill up air-time.)
2. The Past (most of what we know doesn't pass the 'Nullius in verba' test – it's just hearsay. And our memories are dodgy too.)
3. The 95+% of the universe which is Dark Matter – or so we think…

4. Everything happening outside this room.
5. Most of the things happening inside this room, including in my own body.
6. Anything my existing senses are too dull to pick up (and mine are getting duller all the time).
7. Anything I have no senses to register e.g. magnetic fields, UV light &c.
8. Anything my senses do pick up but which my brain filters out before I become conscious of them.
9. What anyone else is thinking. 'The hidden thoughts in other people's heads are the great darkness that surrounds us,' writes Theodore Zeldin.
10. How any of the gazillions of creatures that are not me perceive the world. 'How must it be,' asks Lyanda Lynn Haupt, 'to live guided by flight and fragrance? What manner of intelligence forms within a life shaped and moulded by these things? Or the whisker-based night-seeing of rodents? Or the skin-based knowing of earthworms?'
11. Anything I've just heard from someone else (like the location of Tierra del Fuego) which, without my own verification, may turn out to be a hoax, or just mistaken.
12. Anything we call 'knowing' which is only cerebration. 'Though he can build a stately house, yet he cannot build a honey-comb; and though he can plant a slip, yet he cannot make a tree;' wrote Margaret Cavendish of human pretensions. Four centuries later, entomologists and biologists will tell us they now know how these things are done, but still they cannot do them. A bee that told its

friends it knew how honey-combs were built, but couldn't make one would be laughed out of the hive. Other creatures, innocent of books, laboratories and Wikipedia have no comprehension of our gulf between knowing and doing.

An Incomplete Checklist of Things I Don't Know I Don't Know About

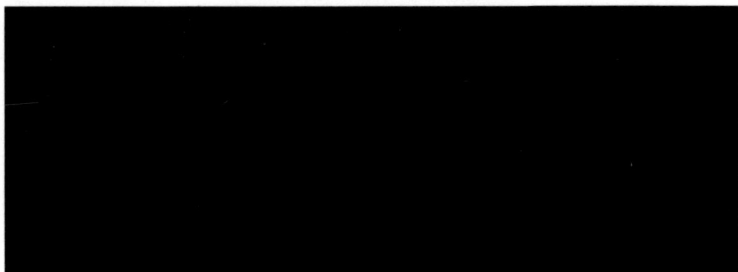

That's quite a lot of ignorance, reaching out to the ends of the universe (and perhaps into other universes), burrowing down into our minds and into the crazy sub-atomic world, surrounding us at everyday level as we misinterpret even the people we know best, stretching into the great unknowns of the future and the past. Our piping dream of total knowledge is receding as fast as the galaxies which, as the expansion of the universe accelerates, will to generations far hence become invisible, and leave our night sky a blank (well, this is what I'm told!) In the circs, it seems absurd to huddle round our little pot of facts.

There is, in any case, a darker side to knowing things. All our knowledge is accompanied by the invisible shadow of our ignorance. When we impose our knowledge, we weaponise this ignorance. Thalidomide, DDT, CFCs, PCBs, microplastics are just some examples of our applied knowledge unleashing the disastrous side-effects of our ignorance. Who knew that our jaunty motoring and dashing conquest of the skies would make the planet uninhabitable? 'A little learning is a dangerous thing' and all our learning in the end is little.

Recognising this requires wisdom rather than data, as the ancient sages understood. Now we admire and give Nobel Prizes to men who study black holes; Confucius, Buddha, St Francis and the rest had other things on their minds. The essence of wisdom is selectivity, sifting what is worth attention (as our brains do naturally). It needs the space and time that an ease with not knowing can give, as a poem needs the whiteness of the page that gnaws round the printed words. The blankness gives room for reflection. Without it, it's just prose.

Our bodies are at ease with ignorance. Most processes happen without our conscious direction; a woman in a coma will give birth when she's due. No cerebration or intellection is required. This is the natural knowledge that the rest of creation relies upon. A rose doesn't need to understand the garden. It, like the rest of us, just needs to do its stuff. Life is the thing, not knowledge. Instead of trying to accumulate data, we could relish the simple but magical fitness of our bodies for this world. That I can, for example, skip down stairs or reach for a glass of wine without accident is proof of the basic affinity between the world as it is and the world as pictured in my brain – the miracles of co-ordination, memory and imagination. Almost too mundane to notice, this is a movingly beautiful thing – the harmony between each of us and our environment, the heartening reassurance we belong here.

Our capacities have of course been wonderfully refined by natural selection, but there is something inherent in all living things that is and always has been in basic consonance with the world – perhaps because life itself sprang from its inanimate surroundings. That first living cell four billion years ago had no needs that could not be met by the place in which it found itself. Organism and environment instantaneously meshed. That is the remarkable fact upon which all history has depended.

This deep affinity with the world contrasts starkly with the information-based cerebral knowledge my laptop wants to foist on me. Our 'ignorance' is not a hindrance – it's an integral part of existence. Accepting it is not grudging resignation, a surly submission to the inevitable, nor is it laziness. It aligns us with reality, humble not cocksure. 'Do the little things,' St David told his disciples. '*Gwnewch y pethau bychain.*'

The ancient Athenians built a shrine 'To the Unknown God'. Perhaps they were just hedging their bets, but there's wisdom in making some kind of obeisance to the vast unknownness that surrounds us.

Quiet country churches are sanctuaries of ignorance. Not error but ***unknowing***. In our hectic world where everyone has, and ceaselessly expresses, opinions, they are formalised spaces where opinion is presumptuous. There may be creeds and commandments on the wall, but silence overmasters them. You could call this 'mystery' if you liked, but that suggests otherworldliness; unknowability is here now and everywhere, a condition of being alive.

The church is no 'holier' than the hill outside, but cloistered within those quiet walls we are denied the horizons which distract us with ambition. The mind is directed by centuries of witness to the presence and constancy of the Whole Thing – unpredictable in its manifestations of droughts and storms, birth and sudden death – but certain in its transcendence of our preening and fretting. There it still is, recognised in the stillness of the cool church, but present too in the woods, on the hill, in the world under your feet, in your body (where billions of our cousin bacteria live their coherent single-celled existences. Zen microbes, beyond attachment and fickle ideas of happiness. Each already knows everything it needs; so, in fact, do we.)

At Rhulen, perhaps the quietest place on earth, the doorway and the altar niche are curiously shaped. It is said that the ignorant peasants there tried to build an arch but got it wrong, never having seen one in this part of Radnorshire. We, in our sophistication, know all about arches but, despite their simplicity and lack of learning, they could see quite plainly the existence of an incomprehensible, controlling power greater than themselves, which is why they built the church in the first place. More clearly than us they knew their ignorance.

STA *
ET * C
ONSI
DERA

SEEINGS – 3

Almost a thousand years ago, late in the year 1039 in England two brothers, the last of the Viking claimants to the throne, plotted to fight and kill one another. A world away in Kyoto, Japan, a lady now known only as 'Takasue's daughter', serving at the court of the infant Princess Yushi, attended the ceremony for the Naming of the Buddhas:

'I set out for home before daybreak the next morning when the snow was coming down in scattered flakes. In the freezing dawn the moon was dimly reflected in the glossy sleeves of my dark red robe, and it seemed to me that the moon's face was wet with tears. These lines came to me:

> Sadly the year is drawing to an end
> And the night is giving way to dawn
> While moonbeams wanly shine upon my sleeve.'

(taken from *As I Crossed a Bridge of Dreams* trans. Ivan Morris 1971)

NIGHT & DAY

God Appears & God is Light
To those poor Souls who dwell in Night
But does a Human Form Display
To those who Dwell in Realms of Day.

Interpreting Blake is a chancy business. Some verses are as simple as they appear, others are booby-trapped. I've read that this one has mystical Swedenborgian overtones, but I think perhaps it has a simpler STA meaning. (Does this mean I am claiming Blake as a proto-STA prophet? It would be fairer to say that I have noticed some things he'd seen already. STA is not a new philosophy, just a new formulation of old, often overlooked, ideas.) Blake seems to be saying that if you can see the goodness of the world around you ('Realms of Day') you can see divinity there; if you cannot, you are forced to imagine that something outside your experience – even contrary to your experience, light in darkness – exists to make amends for the errors of reality.

Much of religion is aimed at these night-owls. A Buddhist tries to escape from the drudgery of samsara, the endless cycle of suffering existence. Jesus too warns us not to trust in the world: there is another place, somewhere over the gravestone, where the manifest ineptitudes and injustices of life will be soothed away. These are seductive tales, justifying us in our discontent, consoling us for our sense of inadequacy by making inadequacy the hallmark of creation. I have no idea whether these spiritual elsewheres are real or not, but they certainly devalue our daily earth-bound activities.

Science too joins the attack. Its astonishing discoveries take us into a realm far removed from our own experience. Quarks are too small, the universe too big, the mathematics too complex, the dark matter too dark for these to be more than adventure tales to astound us. We can perhaps rationalise a Higgs Boson particle, but we cannot feel it as a real thing. Most of us do not climb mountains with clocks to test relativity, nor fire photons at apertures, nor watch for a clumsy neutrino to give itself away by barging into an atom. We have to take these things on trust (if we pay attention at all), rather like medieval peasants hearing rumours from the monasteries of the latest ideas about the Trinity, marvelling briefly at the mysteries of God and education, before turning back to the plough and the fertile earth.

STA is with the peasants. It sees no need to belittle experience. It looks at the lived reality of each moment. This 'Realms of Day' method is essentially that followed by every other living creature, none of which employs an organised church, a heavily-funded scientific establishment or mass media to tell it that what is happening elsewhere is more important than its own experience. There is a danger in disparaging all that surrounds us as unreal, inadequate or merely the by-product of other forces. In real life the wars go on, the greed and bullying and rape and prejudice, and all the petty gracelessness that sours our days. I'm not sure that a God in Heaven or multiverses help much. They may perhaps explain everything; they may perhaps not exist. They're too remote for us to know. The priesthoods, whether religious or scientific, who claim they're telling us the ultimate truth are telling us irrelevancies.

Of course, many from the Celtic saints to Ronald Blythe have seen God through his works, and all scientists are first inspired by curiosity about their surroundings. For many from the pre-Socratics through the Schoolmen to the naturalists in holy orders like Gilbert White and Gregor Mendel, religious and scientific wonder were the same thing. But the tradition of *contemptus mundi* is strong. The fifteenth century poet Sion Cent called the world *hud a lliw*, magic and illusion; the modern neurologist David Eagleman tells us 'the world around you is an illusion, an elaborate show put on by your brain'. These 'poor Souls who dwell in Night' reject the evidence of reality, one rapt by thoughts of heaven, the other wrapped up in himself.

The main gripe against the world is its evanescence. Even its glories are transitory. This is the First Noble Truth of Buddhism and St Paul shares its anxiety ('For here we have no continuing city, but seek one to come.') But permanence does not exist – it is a fantasy invented by those who are frustrated with life's elusiveness and want to pin it down. (Is this, I wonder, a peculiarity of a written rather than oral culture?) Nature has no period, no double bar, no frame, no *FIN*, no dying fall; it is unstoppably changeful. Nor would such a stasis be paradise – it would be more like an Arctic white-out, eternal terrifying sameness. Without impermanence there could be no hope, no growth and no possibility. All the richness of life comes from its changes – the song that is not a monotone, the flower that refuses to remain a seed. STA is thrilled by the constant shocks of mutability, which permeates the most solid-seeming objects. Snowdon was once higher than Everest – a mountain is as fragile as a moth. Look lively. All is flux and demands our quick attention.

We are as changeable as everything else. Some neurologists infer from this that we have no personal identity, but why should fixity be a condition of reality when fixity itself is a fantasy? STA's notion is more flexible: I am still me even if that 'me' changes every second – being and becoming are the same thing.

'Those who dwell in Realms of Day' can see in human form (and equally in tree or flower or elephant since we know from Darwin that we are all related) what Blake calls 'God' and what I, more tentatively, call 'the whole business', the universe particularised in one individual, a tiny but integral and indispensable part of creation.

> The movement on the far side of the river is a flock of lapwing feeding along the bordering field, their plume-crowns fanned out. An unseen interruption and they all rise, an eruption of flickering over bronze clouds. The last of the sun, casting shadows on this mini murmuration. Peewit, peewit. Sprinkling and pulsing wings, they twist around together once before coming to ground again. The sun drops and time slips everywhere, but here it stands still and I can feel the lapwings as if they were all beside me. The world moves so fast, with too little care and too much cruelty. Here,

everything is still and filled with the music of wingbeats, bird calls and the odd human gasp and giggle. The day was all golden, all light, despite the darkening skies around us.

Dara McAnulty, *Diary of a Young Naturalist*

This is not illusory, inadequate or irrelevant. This is wonder unfiltered by screens or media, by expertise, expectation or the superstructures of explanation. No theory, no worry about permanence, no hankering for elsewheres, just the fullness of here and now, experienced and made our own.

ZUM * E
RSTAU
NEN * B
IN * IC
H * DA !

SEEINGS – 4

Goethe's youthful celebrity was fading. He was now a drudge (Inspector of Mines) at the court of Weimar and desperate for glamour. *Kennst du das land, wo die Zitronen blühn.*

Finally, at thirty-seven, he escaped across the Alps and rushed to Venice for his first sight of the sea. The following day he went back, and sat for hours watching crabs and limpets. In his heightened state of expectancy, it was a revelation. "What a splendid thing a living organism is! How precisely fitted to its condition, how true, how *full of being*!" *Wie whar, wie seiend!*

This was a glimpse of the truth he had been looking for – the imperturbable self-sufficiency of these little animals, their necessity in contrast with the folderols of society – toytown Weimar or priest-ridden Italy. His seaside epiphany revealed a different world: 'the firm ground of nature where everyone is only what he is and we all have equal claims'. Such understanding made him 'more solid', he said.

He became addicted to observation – 'I do nothing except look, go away, and come back and look again' – and developed his own limpet-like calm. In revolutionary times Goethe was, as one biographer puts it, 'monumentally normal'.

'I shall never rest until I know that all my ideas are derived, not from hearsay or tradition, but from my real living contact with the things themselves ... I am here to marvel,' Goethe tells our screen-fixated world.

CAT'S EYES

When Phlo sits on my chest, her nose almost touching mine, my brain goes into meltdown. My eyes, my optic nerve and even my cerebral cortex (which should know better) tell me that she has three eyes, then none, then one, or two. Another part of my cerebellum wearily ignores this data-storm and insists that she has two, in spite of the evidence literally staring me in the face. It has used memory, logic and probability to assert its case, and a bit of second-form biology to explain why I am looking at a two-eyed cat with three eyes. Faced with the options of a) a known limitation of stereoscopic vision or b) a shape-shifting creature who can grow or lose her eyes at will, I dully accept option a).

Here I am, a man, a representative of *Homo sapiens* in the Anthropocene Age, the 'highest form of life', 'how noble in reason', 'in apprehension how like a god', and my 'infinite' faculties, honed by billions of years of Natural Selection, are scrambled, my biotech bamboozled by a cat's affection.

It is only because I have a long experience of cats, and three blissful years of co-habitation with Phlo, that a part of my consciousness flagged up the discrepancy, unearthing that memory of biology lessons to explain the fault in the system. Suppose I were looking at something new, some subatomic particle, some phenomenon half a cosmos away. How could I know if it were real or a three-eyed cat?

STA is an initially materialist world-view – not in a

consumerist, possessive, raveningly-destructive way, but because it recognises that the world is made of materia – cats, trees, water, stone – and draws its fundamental knowledge from experience of materia. It does not rely on hypotheses without a material basis, but it doesn't dismiss them either. Some, like the existence of an omniscient divine being, have been so widely believed and so influential, it would be absurdly arrogant to rule them out on the basis of my pipsqueak opinion. Nevertheless STA rests squarely on its foundation of experience. But as I listen to Bach, say, or read Julian's visions, or see the dogged piety of unfashionable church-goers, or even just look at a trinocular cat, I can guess there may be more to this than meets the eye.

Then Phlo settles down and over her head I watch the winter morning sun ignite bare branches of ash and walnut with the softest blue beyond, and I know there's a life's worth of richness within our own experience too.

STA AND 'THE MEANING OF LIFE'

Victor Frankl was an Austrian Jewish psychologist whose theory – the central role of meaning in human life – was tested and ultimately vindicated in the most abhorrent conditions human life has ever endured, Auschwitz.

> "There is nothing in the world, I venture to say, that would so effectively help one to survive even the worst conditions as the knowledge that there is a meaning in one's life. There is much wisdom in the words of Nietzsche: 'He who has a why to live for can bear almost any how' … In the Nazi concentration camps, one could have witnessed that those who knew there was a task waiting for them to fulfil were most apt to survive."

Amidst the physical degradation, he tried to think of the books he would write and the lectures he would give after the war, and survived to found a new school of psychotherapy (logotherapy) and write the generous, humbling little book I have just read, *Man's Search for Meaning*.

That was seventy-five years ago. Things have changed. Google 'the meaning of life' and you get Monty Python. The whole idea is a bit of a joke – but quietly, in secret, we all still wonder about it sometimes.

What might we mean by 'meaning'? I think there are three possible degrees of meaning, shading into one another:

a) what we might call 'cosmic' – the inkling that our lives are part of a universal, even divine, order;

b) a 'whole life' meaning – that, without any religious or cosmic dimension, our personal life nonetheless has a valuable purpose, a shape, and that our individual actions make up a coherent story;

c) immediate meaning – that, without either religion or even the sense of a self, we can find some valid task and do it well. A man may, for example, decide that building a replica of HMS Victory out of matchsticks will give him a purpose. It may not make sense of his whole life but it will give him a motive each morning and stitch one day to the next.

All of the above, though in diminishing degrees, contain the idea of connection – that an action is linked to others, and has a significance beyond itself. This seems to be at the root of 'meaning', but it is open to attack from two sides.

First, as we move from a) to c), so the meaning becomes potentially more arbitrary. Do we commend and envy the Victory builder for his sense of purpose? or do we think 'what a loser'? And what if the cat jumps up and knocks it off the table – can the meaning of life be as fragile as matchwood? If another man says that violence gives meaning to his life, we can be clearer about the limitations of the 'whatever works for you' approach.

Secondly, as we move from c) to a), so the source of the meaning becomes more remote, perhaps even more unreal. Many people reject the idea of a divine order, and some also deny that we have a personal identity which could make sense of a 'whole life' meaning. Meanwhile c) may seem too arbitrary and specific to warrant the term 'meaning' at all.

The monocentric delusion

A devout search for the one true God and rational scepticism about a divine order may seem to be opposite impulses but in fact they have much in common. Both are examples of the tendency, most marked in Western civilisations, to believe that focus and analysis are the paths to truth – that if you delve into the heart of something, get down to brass tacks, the nitty-gritty, the nub of the question, you will find the answer, whether it be God, a 'God particle' or an absence. Science has, from its earliest days, been guided by the notion that analysis – reducing things to their smallest components – will reveal the truth, and so we keep searching, wondering if there are littler particles than the littlest we've found so far. There are problems with this approach. Analysis is, quite literally, 'breaking something'. It isolates organisms – bacteria, plants or monkeys – in laboratories, pretending that their wider, native environment is a distraction rather than their vital nutriment. It acts as though the world were made of pieces that could be studied separately, then bolted together like a bicycle. 'Focus', which is always used as a positive word in English, could equally well be defined as 'blinding yourself to most of what is around you'. To focus is to prejudge what is worth your attention before you begin to look.

This centralising habit appears in Western Art too – the sitter looming out of a grunge of unimportantness; composition which establishes a hierarchy of significance; perspective which fawns on the viewer. The Classical tradition builds symmetries around a central line or point, striving for a harmony and order which it believes exists in heaven or mathematics or anywhere other than the messy reality of experience.

This intellectual ideal, and then the coincidence of a monotheistic religion (Christianity) arising just when the West was ruled by a single power (Rome) cemented in our culture the idea that order is monocentric. This view always seeks a single authority: the Ultimate Cause, the philosopher's stone or the theory of everything which would, as Stephen Hawking said, reveal to us 'the mind of God'. Douglas Adams, famously and brilliantly, ridicules millennia of earnest monocentrism: the answer is 42 !

Reality is not monocentric; the centre is everywhere. There is unity – we are all related, all made of the same stuff – but just as importantly, there is diversity – we are all unique. Each of us is inescapably the centre of our universe. We cannot relate to anything except through our own perceptions. Yet we know that every other creature is equally a centre no less valid or important than ours. It is not that there is no centre, but that everything is the centre. Nor is there any hierarchy. The bottom of a hedge in Painscastle is as much the hub of the world as Rome, Jerusalem or New York. The stone in the sub-base of the High Street is as holy as the Black Stone in Mecca – it is our cultural traditions that assign them different value. 'Meaning' then is less likely to be found in a single point – like an X on a treasure-map – than to be an element in everything in this polycentric universe.

Making sense

Monocentrism is a local, cultural (Western) tradition; scepticism too is learnt behaviour – biologically we are 'meaning-seeking creatures'. This is not merely to say that we find comfort in symmetry and like stories to have a resolution (though Christopher Booker in *The Seven Basic Plots* makes a good case for the psychological need for such completeness). It is to say that we literally 'make sense' of the world by finding patterns, discerning shapes and linking together millions of bits of data that flood into our brains to build something coherent, a story about our surroundings that enables us to live in them.

If I tap you on the arm, smile and say 'Coffee?' your ears hear my voice (amidst all the background noise), your eyes see the smile, nerve receptors feel the touch. These processes are entirely independent of one another. Only when all this disparate information reaches your brain is it sifted, reconstituted and interpreted. Then you recognise that the various actions are signals, you link them together, match them to other experiences in your memory and give them a meaning – hopefully the same meaning I intended to transmit. All of this before the more conscious rational/psychological evaluation of my motives, and the further social/emotional/even financial judgement about the desirability of coffee or my company. Our most basic mental function then is seeking meaning. We 'make sense' of the world in the faith that the sense we make mirrors the external reality. We cannot drink a cup of tea or jump on a bus without this unceasing process of meaning-making.

At this point it becomes clear that 'meaning' cannot be a solely human business. The fundamental fact of evolution is that all organisms are related. All share a common ancestry; all make sense of their surroundings in the same way – they receive information and act upon it. The 'meaning of life' therefore cannot be purely a matter of intellect, because most creatures do not share that particular evolutionary refinement. The universe did not lie meaningless for billions of years until some old Greeks started asking questions. We (especially academics and writers) like to suppose that rational thought is the supreme quality in the cosmos, partly because it is *Homo sapiens'* party-piece and partly because the language with which we discuss such matters is itself intellectual, consciously constructed in the wake of thoughts and feelings. But our advanced intellects do not make humans exceptional; we are an integral part of nature and it would be presumptuous of us to suppose that our special characteristic must be the one that governs the universe, and a better mechanism for understanding it than any other creature's. So a general question about the 'meaning of life' must be equally applicable to a dormouse or a dandelion as to you or me. Which perhaps is unexpected.

If there is a 'meaning of life' it cannot be an intellectual puzzle. We are physical, emotional, perhaps spiritual beings too. Our actions are rarely purely intellectual. Most of our essential work – breathing, digesting, &c – is done without troubling our conscious minds at all. Our intellect is like a CEO or Head of an NHS Trust fussing with busyness and self-importance while the vital stuff is done by workers who get on much better for being ignored by the boss. Try using your conscious mind to laugh, sweat or heal a cut and you'll see how hopeless it is; if our consciousness were really in charge, we'd all be dead. It mostly busies itself instead with social, political, cultural affairs. Fascinating as these sometimes are, the meaning of life is not to be found in such *divertissements*.

In Auschwitz, Frankl met the same limitations:

> 'We needed to stop asking about the meaning of life, and instead to think of ourselves as those who were being questioned by life – daily and hourly. Our answer must consist, not in talk and meditation, but in right action and right conduct. Life ultimately means taking the responsibility to find the right answer to its problems and to fulfil the tasks which it constantly sets for each individual. These tasks, and therefore the meaning of life, differ from man to man, and from moment to moment.'

Right action

Each of us (and each dormouse and dandelion too) can act in tune with the meaning of our lives. The problems that seemed to bedevil the idea of meaning – unreality at one extreme, arbitrariness at the other – do not apply once we have understood the reality of the polycentric universe. Because we are already connected to everything that is, the distinction between 'cosmic' and 'immediate' evaporates. Meaning does not rely on remote gods, nor need our local actions be arbitrary (unless we choose to turn inwards and make a fetish of individualism).

It seems likely that a dandelion and even a dormouse have little or no choice about what they do – for them right action is inherent and inevitable. A dandelion cannot err. We, however, are in a constant tizzy, badgered by uncertainty, worry, guilt, heir to an embarrassment of possibilities. What is 'right action' for a human? The specific detail, as Frankl said, must vary from moment to moment but STA perhaps can give some general guidance. The world is neither monolithic nor atomised; it is a mass of diverse elements forming a single unity (just like a view from a hilltop, a piece of music, a film, ourselves). Right action must acknowledge these basic facts of our simultaneous uniqueness and interdependence. STA's Four Natural Duties meet the criteria. They are haecceity, awareness, love and creativity – the exercise of our uniqueness, our alertness to, and wise concern for, our surroundings, and our expression of the creativity evident in all living things.

These are mostly self-explanatory but haecceity needs to be distinguished from individuation. 'Individual' literally means 'indivisible' – a useful word to emphasise that the self exists and has its own unity. But it is often represented as though individuality were fixed and had a line drawn around it separating it from every other individual. The word also encourages a dangerously introspective focus – the striving to 'Know Thyself' as though we can study ourselves in isolation, like a lab rat cut off from its environment. By contrast, haecceity – the unique but multifarious and ever-changing identity of each of us – finds itself by looking outwards, and reacting without pre-conceptions to whatever it finds. We are not fixed characters; we are what we do.

In Tolstoy's *Resurrection* a nameless old tramp explains his philosophy: "Many faiths there be, but the Spirit is one. In you an' in me, an' in 'im. That means, if any man of us believes in the Spirit within 'im, us'll all be united. Let everyone be 'imself, and us'll all be one." Our shared experience of uniqueness binds us together, just as does our physical relatedness. So too does our deep interdependence. None of us has developed in isolation. As Ted Hughes's Hawk says, 'It took the whole of Creation/To produce my foot, my each feather'. Coincidentally, in the same year those lines were written, the meteorologist Edward Lorenz discovered the chaos theory which validated Hughes's intuition. Infinitesimal changes somewhere in the Earth's past could have produced a very different foot or feather, or a different us because *each of us is the product of everything that has happened, particularized at this time and in this place.* Evolutionary family trees – those spidery, skeletal diagrams – tell only a fraction of the story. 'It took the whole of Creation.' We are both completely connected and entirely unique.

The fullness of that connection demands the engagement of all our attributes – our senses and instincts, our spirit and emotions, our intellect – with everyone and everything we meet, so that we can understand them more completely and can perceive through them their own connection to the holicity of the world. With this fullness of connection none of our actions need ever be arbitrary. Haecceity means that each of us feels sensations and thinks thoughts slightly differently from any other creature in history.

Every single experience, however humdrum, is an exploration of uncharted territory, no duplication ever occurs. Thus the total sum of experience in the world is always increasing. Everything we do expands the universe.

When I was a kid I was very proud to be Welsh. I did not think Wales existentially better than Scotland, Italy, Afghanistan &c (though it was evidently better than England), but I felt a connection to the place and culture, a recognition of its preciousness and a loyalty to it. When in my early twenties I moved to London, I felt a similar pride at being part of the great metropolis – the river, the history, the galleries and theatres. I explored the streets excited by the sizzling possibilities and the sense that all this – by no means exclusively – was mine.

That feeling survives but infinitely expanded. Although I have only the most rudimentary knowledge of botany or cosmology, I can enjoy the lichen under my feet and the galaxies above my head and literally everything in between, recognising our connection, our kinship – the biological relationship with all living things, the material relationship with all things animate or inanimate. I can relish the ancient trees, the sunsets, the kingfishers and all the bobby-dazzlers that get their pictures on to screensavers, but I give the slugs and the liverworts a nod too, acknowledging that we are together a part of the whole thing, citizens of the holicity. It is in this cosmic patriotism, this belonging, this inescapable involvement in all things, that I suspect the latent meaning of life can be found.

I am as integral to the cosmos as the sun – qualitatively speaking.

(From a quantitative point of view the sun is obviously rather more important and influential.) At this moment the universe would not be all that it could be without my sensations, my thoughts, the infinitesimal influence of my presence; I complete it. When I die, I (if there is still an 'I') or the bits formerly known as me will continue to be an essential component. The same, of course, goes for all of us – no competition, no hierarchy. Is this not meaning enough? and incentive enough to be wholly engaged?

We might flip Mephistopheles: 'why this is heaven nor am I out of it' – not a hard-won, after-death paradise of changeless, pain-free bliss with nothing to fear and nothing to hope for, communing with the Everything for all eternity, but here – an ever-changing fullness of experience (bliss and pain, fear and hope included) communing with everything.

Living is as instinct with meaning as our bodies with DNA. We do not need to look for it but to see it. Not a quest but a change of perspective. 'You never enjoy the world aright till the Sea itself floweth in your veins, till you are clothed with the heavens, and crowned with the stars: and perceive yourself to be the sole heir of the whole world, and more than so, because men are in it who are every one sole heirs as well as you.' (Traherne) Dormice and dandelions too.

Is this right? that being ourselves and taking part can be said to be the meaning of our lives? I think so. At any rate, it's as close to 'right' as I can get at the moment, though that's not saying a lot. (And, of course, it doesn't attempt to explain the meaning, purpose or significance, if any, of the universe itself – that must always be beyond our experience and capacities.) Anyway, whether I am right or wrong needn't matter much to anyone else because, as Frankl writes, 'each man is questioned by life; and he can only answer to life by answering for his own life'. We can and should enlarge our minds and explore new possibilities by studying the thoughts of others with what Bertrand Russell calls 'a kind of hypothetical sympathy, until it is possible to know what it feels like to believe in [their] theories' – a philosophy is something you live, not something you think – but we cannot rely on anyone else's authority or opinion. We have to work it out for ourselves. Sta et considera miracula – stop, and have a think about these wonderful things.

Some months after finishing this, I found a draft across which I'd written (perhaps after a glass or two of wine) "I wish I could believe what I know".

ACKNOWLEDGEMENTS

Thanks most of all to Graeme Hobbs for designing and setting the text, for creating the four beautiful letterpress inscriptions and, with Mary, for the encouragement and support without which this would have remained a folder of unread computer files. Visit *fallowpages.art* for more of Graeme's letterpress work.

Tortoise was printed and bound by Orphans Press Ltd, Leominster. I'm very grateful to Katie Shearer and Mark Jenner for their patient helpfulness.

Printed in Garamond on Arena Milk paper with Rives Tradition Natural Rough cover.

Published by The Cyrus Press
gareth@sta-website.com

ISBN 978-1-3999-4310-9

Second impression

sta-website.com

STA is a way of looking at the world rather than an intellectual and verbal argument. The website offers a visual alternative to the more literary approach of this book and the serial (below). It's unhurried, unexpected, playful & rather odd.

sta-serial.com

The original book *STA* was lavishly illustrated and is therefore sadly too expensive to republish. Here it is issued free online in short sections from October 2022, until the whole text is available.

Some reviews of *STA*:

'A hugely readable, empathetic and ingenious braiding of philosophy, poetry, art and history brought together with a love for the natural world to show how we might yet exist alongside it more fully'.
Owen Sheers

'I am a great believer in STA. It is more than a book and has enriched my life deeply'. Max Porter

'A true, personal and still-private statement from the heart in a way few books manage. Its philosophy is integral to the life of the man who wrote it so that STA, in the great and long tradition of English memoir, remains a shrine to thoughtfulness and the rich, neglected virtues of reflection.' Adam Nicolson